Cool Ships
USS Shiloh CG 67
US Navy Guided Missile Cruiser

Nimble Books LLC

DEDICATION

To the ships and sailors of the U.S. Navy past, present, and future.

CONTENTS

TABLE OF CONTENTS

INTRODUCTION

This curated collection of 169 high-resolution color images related to the US Navy guided missile cruiser *USS Shiloh* CG 67, captured by US armed forces personnel from 2015 to 2020, illustrates the life of a modern ship and its sailors in all their variety.

IMAGES

Seaman Apprentice Michelle Salinas, from Mesquite, Texas, brings in a line aboard Ticonderoga-class guided-missile cruiser USS Shiloh (CG 67) as the ship departs Fleet Activities Yokosuka. Shiloh is on patrol in the 7th Fleet area of responsibility supporting security and stability in the Indo-Asia-Pacific region. (U.S. Navy photo by Mass Communication Specialist Seaman Abby Rader/Released)

Arleigh Burke-class guided-missile destroyer USS Stethem (DDG 63) transits alongside Ticonderoga-class guided-missile cruiser USS Shiloh (CG 67) as it returns to Fleet Activities Yokosuka. Shiloh is on patrol in the 7th Fleet area of responsibility supporting security and stability in the Indo-Asia-Pacific region. (U.S. Navy photo by Mass Communication Specialist Seaman Abby Rader/Released)

Gunner's Mate 1st Class Talbot Crispin, left, from Spokane, Wash., instructs Cryptologic Technician (Collection) 3rd Class Trevel Dixon, from Jamaica Queens, N.Y., during a 9MM small arms handling qualification course aboard Ticonderoga-class guided-missile cruiser USS Shiloh (CG 67). Shiloh is on patrol in the 7th Fleet area of responsibility supporting of security and stability in the Indo-Asia-Pacific region. (U.S. Navy photo by Mass Communication Specialist Seaman Abby Rader/Released)

Sailors assigned to Ticonderoga-class guided-missile cruiser USS Shiloh (CG 67) participate in a 9mm naval handling qualification course. Shiloh is on patrol in the 7th Fleet area of responsibility supporting of security and stability in the Indo-Asia-Pacific region. (U.S. Navy photo by Mass Communication Specialist Seaman Abby Rader/Released)

Seaman Adolphus Umoja, from Willingboro, N.J., stands watch aboard Ticonderoga-class guided-missile cruiser USS Shiloh (CG 67). Shiloh is on patrol in the 7th Fleet area of responsibility supporting of security and stability in the Indo-Asia-Pacific region. (U.S. Navy photo by Mass Communication Specialist Seaman Abby Rader/Released)

Boatswain's Mate 3rd Class Nathan Burnau, from Barstow, Calif., prepares for a replenishment-at-sea aboard Ticonderoga-class guided-missile cruiser USS Shiloh (CG 67). Shiloh is on patrol with the George Washington Carrier Strike Group supporting of security and stability in the Indo-Asia-Pacific region. (U.S. Navy photo by Mass Communication Specialist Seaman Abby Rader/Released)

Sailors participate in a replenishment-at-sea aboard Ticonderoga-class guided-missile cruiser USS Shiloh (CG 67). Shiloh is on patrol with the George Washington Carrier Strike Group supporting of security and stability in the Indo-Asia-Pacific region. (U.S. Navy photo by Mass Communication Specialist Seaman Abby Rader/Released)

Boatswain's Mate 3rd Class John Sutcliffe, from Philadelphia, participates in a replenishment-at-sea aboard Ticonderoga-class guided-missile cruiser USS Shiloh (CG 67). Shiloh is on patrol with the George Washington Carrier Strike Group supporting of security and stability in the Indo-Asia-Pacific region. (U.S. Navy photo by Mass Communication Specialist Seaman Abby Rader/Released)

Gunner's Mate 2nd Class Kyle Kloety, from West Bend, Wis., leads the visit, board, search and seizure (VBSS) team assigned to Ticonderoga-class guided-missile cruiser USS Shiloh (CG 67) during VBSS drills. Shiloh is on patrol with the George Washington Carrier Strike Group supporting of security and stability in the Indo-Asia-Pacific region. (U.S. Navy photo by Mass Communication Specialist Seaman Abby Rader/Released)

Fire Controlman 3rd Class Angus Heimen, from Longmont, Colo., participates in a visit, board, search and seizure (VBSS) drill aboard Ticonderoga-class guided-missile cruiser USS Shiloh (CG 67). Shiloh is on patrol with the George Washington Carrier Strike Group supporting of security and stability in the Indo-Asia-Pacific region. (U.S. Navy photo by Mass Communication Specialist Seaman Abby Rader/Released)

Gunner's Mate 2nd Class Kyle Kloety, from West Bend, Wis., participates in a visit, board, search and seizure (VBSS) drill aboard Ticonderoga-class guided-missile cruiser USS Shiloh (CG 67). Shiloh is on patrol with the George Washington Carrier Strike Group supporting of security and stability in the Indo-Asia-Pacific region. (U.S. Navy photo by Mass Communication Specialist Seaman Abby Rader/Released)

Culinary Specialist Seaman Joseph Aniel, from Fort Lauderdale, Fla., middle, shoots a .50-caliber machine gun while Chief Gunner's Mate Rebecca Jasper, from Massillon, Ohio, left, and Gunner's Mate 1st Class Talbot Crispin, from Spokane, Wash., supervise during a live-fire exercise aboard Ticonderoga-class guided-missile cruiser USS Shiloh (CG 67). Shiloh is on patrol with the George Washington Carrier Strike Group supporting security and stability in the Indo-Asia-Pacific region. (U.S. Navy photo by Mass Communication Specialist Seaman Abby Rader/Released)

Logistics Specialist 2nd Class Mcquester Taylor, front, from Dallas, shoots a .50-caliber machine gun while Chief Gunner's Mate Loron Green supervises during a live-fire exercise aboard Ticonderoga-class guided-missile cruiser USS Shiloh (CG 67). Shiloh is on patrol with the George Washington Carrier Strike Group supporting security and stability in the Indo-Asia-Pacific region. (U.S. Navy photo by Mass Communication Specialist Seaman Abby Rader/Released)

Chief Gunner's Mate Rebecca Jasper, from Massillon, Ohio, left, instructs Ship's Serviceman 3rd Class Baichuan Qiao, from Queens, N.Y., during a .50-caliber machine gun live-fire exercise aboard Ticonderoga-class guided-missile cruiser USS Shiloh (CG 67). Shiloh is on patrol with the George Washington Carrier Strike Group supporting security and stability in the Indo-Asia-Pacific region. (U.S. Navy photo by Mass Communication Specialist Seaman Abby Rader/Released)

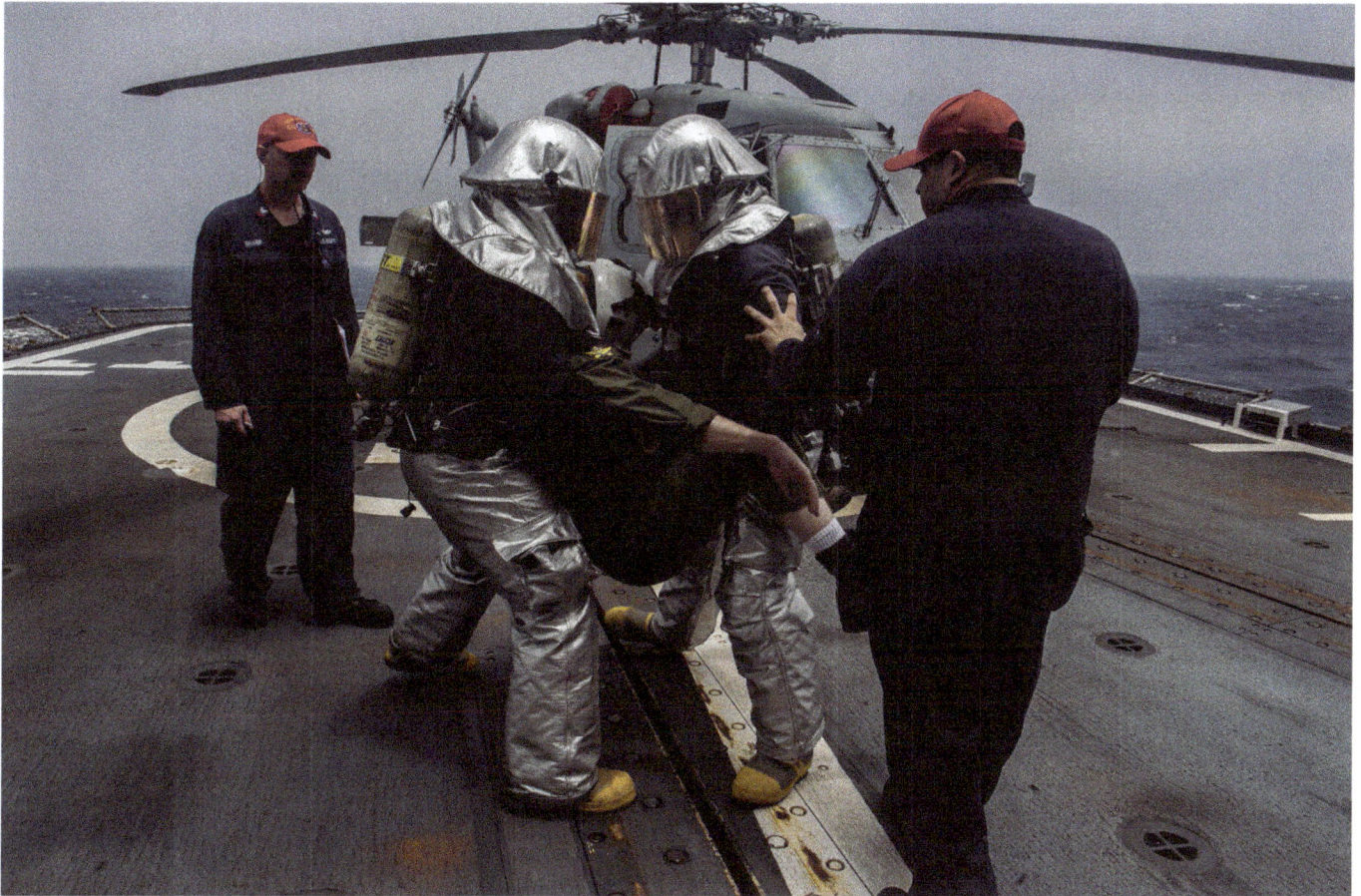

Sailors assigned to Ticonderoga-class guided-missile cruiser USS Shiloh (CG 67) carry a simulated casualty to safety during a crash and salvage drill on the flight deck. Shiloh is on patrol with the George Washington Carrier Strike Group supporting of security and stability in the Indo-Asia-Pacific region. (U.S. Navy photo by Mass Communication Specialist Seaman Abby Rader/Released)

Sailors assigned to Ticonderoga-class guided-missile cruiser USS Shiloh (CG 67) operate a fire hose during a crash and salvage drill on the flight deck. Shiloh is on patrol with the George Washington Carrier Strike Group supporting of security and stability in the Indo-Asia-Pacific region. (U.S. Navy photo by Mass Communication Specialist Seaman Abby Rader/Released)

Sailors and Midshipmen aboard to Ticonderoga-class guided-missile cruiser USS Shiloh (CG 67) man the rails as the ship arrives in Busan for a port visit. Shiloh is on patrol with the George Washington Carrier Strike Group supporting of security and stability in the Indo-Asia-Pacific region. (U.S. Navy photo released by Mass Communication Specialist Seaman Abby Rader/Released)

Sailors assigned to Ticonderoga-class guided-missile cruiser USS Shiloh (CG 67) man the rails as the ship arrives in Busan for a port visit. Shiloh is on patrol with the George Washington Carrier Strike Group supporting of security and stability in the Indo-Asia-Pacific region. (U.S. Navy photo released by Mass Communication Specialist Seaman Abby Rader/Released)

Capt. Kurush Morris, commanding officer of Ticonderoga-class guided-missile cruiser USS Shiloh (CG 67), receives a lei from a Republic of Korean child during a welcoming ceremony after arriving in Busan for a port visit. Shiloh is on patrol with the George Washington Carrier Strike Group supporting of security and stability in the Indo-Asia-Pacific region. (U.S. Navy photo released by Mass Communication Specialist Seaman Abby Rader/Released)

Capt. Kurush Morris, commanding officer of the Ticonderoga-class guided-missile cruiser USS Shiloh (CG 67), briefs Republic of Korea navy Sailors on the capabilities of Shiloh's two embarked MH-60R Seahawk helicopters. Shiloh is on patrol with the George Washington Carrier Strike Group supporting security and stability in the Indo-Asia-Pacific region. (U.S. Navy photo by Ensign William McGough/Released)

Capt. Kurush Morris, left, commanding officer of the Ticonderoga-class guided-missile cruiser USS Shiloh (CG 67), briefs Republic of Korea Navy Capt Youn Jong-Il, commodore, Maritime Task Squadron (MTS) 71, during a tour of Shiloh's combat information center. Shiloh is on patrol with the George Washington Carrier Strike Group supporting security and stability in the Indo-Asia-Pacific region. (U.S. Navy photo by Ensign William McGough/Released)

Gunner's Mate 2nd Class Michael Lucas, from San Francisco, participates in a sea and anchor evolution during a sea and anchor evolution aboard Ticonderoga-class guided-missile cruiser USS Shiloh (CG 67) as the ship departs Busan after a 4-day port visit. Shiloh is on patrol with the George Washington Carrier Strike Group supporting of security and stability in the Indo-Asia-Pacific region. (U.S. Navy photo by Mass Communication Specialist Seaman Abby Rader/Released)

Chief Quartermaster Sam Patel, from Los Angeles, makes an announcement over the announcement system during a sea and anchor evolution aboard Ticonderoga-class guided-missile cruiser USS Shiloh (CG 67) as the ship departs Busan after a 4-day port visit. Shiloh is on patrol with the George Washington Carrier Strike Group supporting of security and stability in the Indo-Asia-Pacific region. (U.S. Navy photo by Mass Communication Specialist Seaman Abby Rader/Released)

Rear Adm. Kim Jong-Il, commander Maritime Task Flotilla (MTF) 7, examines the collar device of a midshipman during a visit to the Ticonderoga-class guided-missile cruiser USS Shiloh (CG 67). Shiloh is on patrol with the George Washington Carrier Strike Group in support of security and stability in the Indo-Asia-Pacific region. (U.S. Navy photo by Fire Controlman 1st Class Kristopher Horton/Released)

Capt. Kurush F. Morris, left, commanding officer of the Ticonderoga-class guided-missile cruiser USS Shiloh (CG 67), explains the function of the combat information center to Rear Adm. Kim Jong-Il, commander Maritime Task Flotilla (MTF) 7, during a visit to Shiloh. Shiloh is on patrol with the George Washington Carrier Strike Group in support of security and stability in the Indo-Asia-Pacific region. (U.S. Navy photo by Fire Controlman 1st Class Kristopher Horton/Released)

Capt. Kurush F. Morris, left, commanding officer of the Ticonderoga-class guided-missile cruiser USS Shiloh (CG 67), explains the function of the combat information center to Rear Adm. Kim Jong-Il, right, commander Maritime Task Flotilla (MTF) 7, during a visit to Shiloh. Shiloh is on patrol with the George Washington Carrier Strike Group in support of security and stability in the Indo-Asia-Pacific region. (U.S. Navy photo by Fire Controlman 1st Class Kristopher Horton/Released)

Capt. Kurush Morris, middle, commanding officer of Ticonderoga-class guided-missile cruiser USS Shiloh (CG 67), discusses the purpose of the navigation bridge to members of the Republic of Korea navy during a tour of Shiloh. Shiloh is on patrol with the George Washington Carrier Strike Group supporting of security and stability in the Indo-Asia-Pacific region. (U.S. Navy photo by Mass Communication Specialist Seaman Abby Rader/Released)

Gen. Curtis Scaparrotti, commander, U.S. Forces Korea, right, talks with Capt. Kurush F. Morris, commanding officer of the Ticonderoga-class guided-missile cruiser USS Shiloh (CG 67), during a ship tour. Shiloh is on Patrol with the George Washington Strike Group in support of security and stability in the Indo-Asia-Pacific region. (U.S. Navy photo by Fire Controlman First Class Kristopher Horton/Released)

Capt. Kurush F. Morris, commanding officer of the Ticonderoga-class guided-missile cruiser USS Shiloh (CG 67), left, Adm. Choi Yoon-Hee, chairman, Republic Of Korea Armed Forces Joint Chiefs Of Staff, center, and Gen. Curtis Scaparrotti, commander, U.S. Forces Korea, discuss ship tactics in the combat information center during a ship tour. Shiloh is on Patrol with the George Washington Strike Group in support of security and stability in the Indo-Asia-Pacific region. (U.S. Navy photo by Fire Controlman First Class Kristopher Horton/Released)

Capt. Kurush F. Morris, commanding officer of the Ticonderoga-class guided-missile cruiser USS Shiloh (CG 67), right, Gen. Curtis Scaparrotti, commander, U.S. Forces Korea, center and Adm. Choi Yoon-Hee, chairman, Republic Of Korea Armed Forces Joint Chiefs Of Staff, discuss ship maneuvers in the bridge during a ship tour. Shiloh is on Patrol with the George Washington Strike Group in support of security and stability in the Indo-Asia-Pacific region. (U.S. Navy photo by Fire Controlman First Class Kristopher Horton/Released)

Gen. Curtis Scaparrotti, commander, U.S. Forces Korea, right, talks with Capt. Kurush F. Morris, commanding officer of the Ticonderoga-class guided-missile cruiser USS Shiloh (CG 67), during a ship tour. Shiloh is on Patrol with the George Washington Strike Group in support of security and stability in the Indo-Asia-Pacific region. (U.S. Navy photo by Fire Controlman First Class Kristopher Horton/Released)

Seaman Apprentice Adolphus Umoja, from Liberia, assigned to the Ticonderoga-class guided-missile cruiser USS Shiloh (CG 67) and other Sailors and Marines stand at attention for the parading of the colors during a naturalization ceremony held at Fleet Activities Yokosuka. Shiloh is assigned to Commander, Task Force 70, and is forward deployed to Yokosuka, Japan, to support security and stability of the Indo-Asia-Pacific region. (U.S. Navy photo by Fire Controlman First Class Kristopher Horton/Released)

Sailors and Marines assigned to various commands at Fleet Activities Yokosuka, take the Oath of Allegiance, to become U.S. citizens, during a naturalization ceremony. (U.S. Navy Photo by Fire Controlman First Class Kristopher Horton/Released)

Seaman Apprentice Adolphus Umoja, from Liberia, right, assigned to the Ticonderoga-class guided-missile cruiser USS Shiloh (CG 67) participates in an interview after becoming a U.S. citizen at a naturalization ceremony held at Fleet Activities Yokosuka. Shiloh is assigned to Commander, Task Force 70, and is forward deployed to Yokosuka, Japan, to support security and stability of the Indo-Asia-Pacific region. (U.S. Navy photo by Fire Controlman First Class Kristopher Horton/Released)

Sailors assigned to the Ticonderoga-class guided-missile cruiser USS Shiloh (CG 67) fire M9 service pistols on the flight deck during a weapons qualification. Shiloh is on patrol with the George Washington Carrier Strike Group supporting security and stability in the Indo-Asia-Pacific region. (U.S. Navy photo by Mass Communication Specialist Kevin V. Cunningham/Released)

Sailors assigned to the Ticonderoga-class guided-missile cruiser USS Shiloh (CG 67) fire M9 service pistols on the flight deck during a weapons qualification. Shiloh is on patrol with the George Washington Carrier Strike Group supporting security and stability in the Indo-Asia-Pacific region. (U.S. Navy photo by Mass Communication Specialist Kevin V. Cunningham/Released)

Sailors assigned to the Ticonderoga-class guided-missile cruiser USS Shiloh (CG 67) fire M9 service pistols on the flight deck during a weapons qualification. Shiloh is on patrol with the George Washington Carrier Strike Group supporting security and stability in the Indo-Asia-Pacific region. (U.S. Navy photo by Mass Communication Specialist Kevin V. Cunningham/Released)

Ship's Serviceman 3rd Class Baichuan Qiao, from New York, takes the Navy-wide petty officer second class exam on the mess decks aboard the Ticonderoga-class guided-missile cruiser USS Shiloh (CG 67). Shiloh is on patrol with the George Washington Carrier Strike Group supporting security and stability in the Indo-Asia-Pacific region. (U.S. Navy photo by Mass Communication Specialist 3rd Class Kevin V. Cunningham/Released)

Hull Technician 2nd Class Colby H. Phipps takes part in a fire drill aboard the Ticonderoga-class guided-missile cruiser USS Shiloh (CG 67). Shiloh is on patrol with the George Washington Carrier Strike Group supporting security and stability in the Indo-Asia-Pacific region. (U.S. Navy photo by Mass Communication Specialist 3rd Class Kevin V. Cunningham/Released)

Hull Technician 2nd Class Colby H. Phipps takes part in a fire drill aboard the Ticonderoga-class guided-missile cruiser USS Shiloh (CG 67). Shiloh is on patrol with the George Washington Carrier Strike Group supporting security and stability in the Indo-Asia-Pacific region. (U.S. Navy photo by Mass Communication Specialist 3rd Class Kevin V. Cunningham/Released)

Damage Controlman 3rd Class Shane D. Leishman-Heim takes part in a fire drill aboard the Ticonderoga-class guided-missile cruiser USS Shiloh (CG 67). Shiloh is on patrol with the George Washington Carrier Strike Group supporting security and stability in the Indo-Asia-Pacific region. (U.S. Navy photo by Mass Communication Specialist 3rd Class Kevin V. Cunningham/Released)

Sailors assigned to the Ticonderoga-class guided-missile cruiser USS Shiloh (CG 67) participate in a fire drill during general quarters. Shiloh is on patrol with the George Washington Carrier Strike Group supporting security and stability in the Indo-Asia-Pacific region. (U.S. Navy photo by Mass Communication Specialist 3rd Class Kevin V. Cunningham/Released)

Sailors assigned to the Ticonderoga-class guided-missile cruiser USS Shiloh (CG 67) participate in a fire drill during general quarters. Shiloh is on patrol with the George Washington Carrier Strike Group supporting security and stability in the Indo-Asia-Pacific region. (U.S. Navy photo by Mass Communication Specialist 3rd Class Kevin V. Cunningham/Released)

Rear Adm. Mark Montgomery, Commander, Battle Force 7th Fleet, addresses the crew of the Ticonderoga-class guided-missile cruiser USS Shiloh (CG 67) over the ship's announcing system during a visit to the ship. Shiloh is on patrol with the George Washington Carrier Strike Group supporting security and stability in the Indo-Asia-Pacific region. (U.S. Navy photo by Mass Communication Specialist 3rd Class Kevin V. Cunningham/Released)

Rear Adm. Mark Montgomery, Commander of Battle Force U.S. 7th Fleet, speaks with Capt. Kurush Morris, commanding officer of the Ticonderoga-class guided-missile cruiser USS Shiloh (CG 67), in the pilot-house during a visit to the ship. Shiloh is on patrol with the George Washington Carrier Strike Group supporting security and stability in the Indo-Asia-Pacific region. (U.S. Navy photo by Mass Communication Specialist 3rd Class Kevin V. Cunningham/Released)

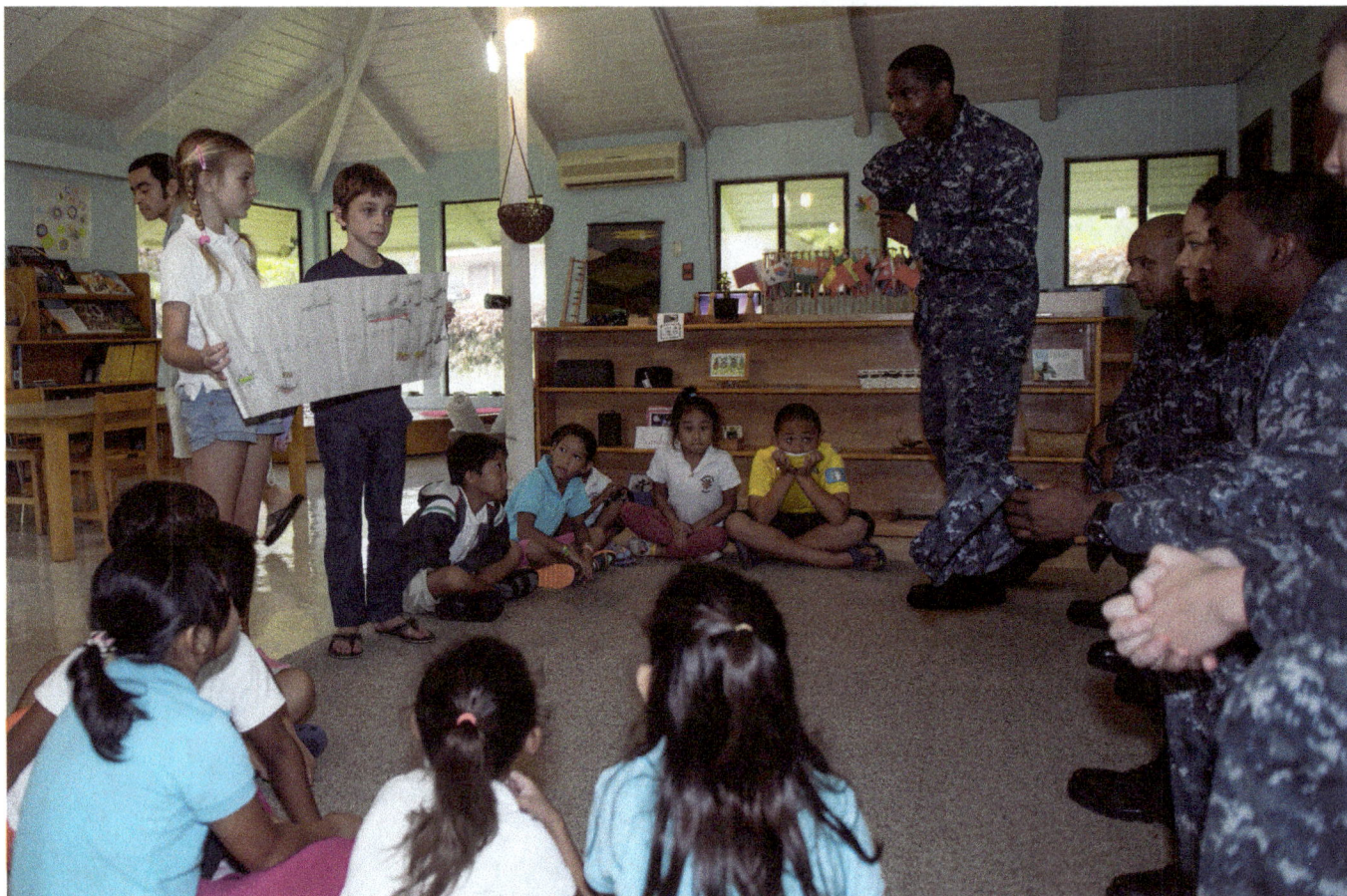

Students from the Brilliant Star Montessori School in Saipan present a drawing of Navy ships to Sailors assigned to the Ticonderoga-class guided-missile cruiser USS Shiloh (CG 67) during a cultural exchange. Shiloh is in Saipan for a scheduled port visit after participating in Valiant Shield, a U.S.-only exercise integrating 18,000 U.S. Navy, Air Force, Army, and Marine Corps personnel, more than 200 aircraft and 19 surface ships, offering real-world joint operational experience to develop capabilities that provide a full range of options to defend U.S. interests and those if its allies and partners. (U.S. Navy photo by Mass Communication Specialist 3rd Class Kevin V. Cunningham/Released)

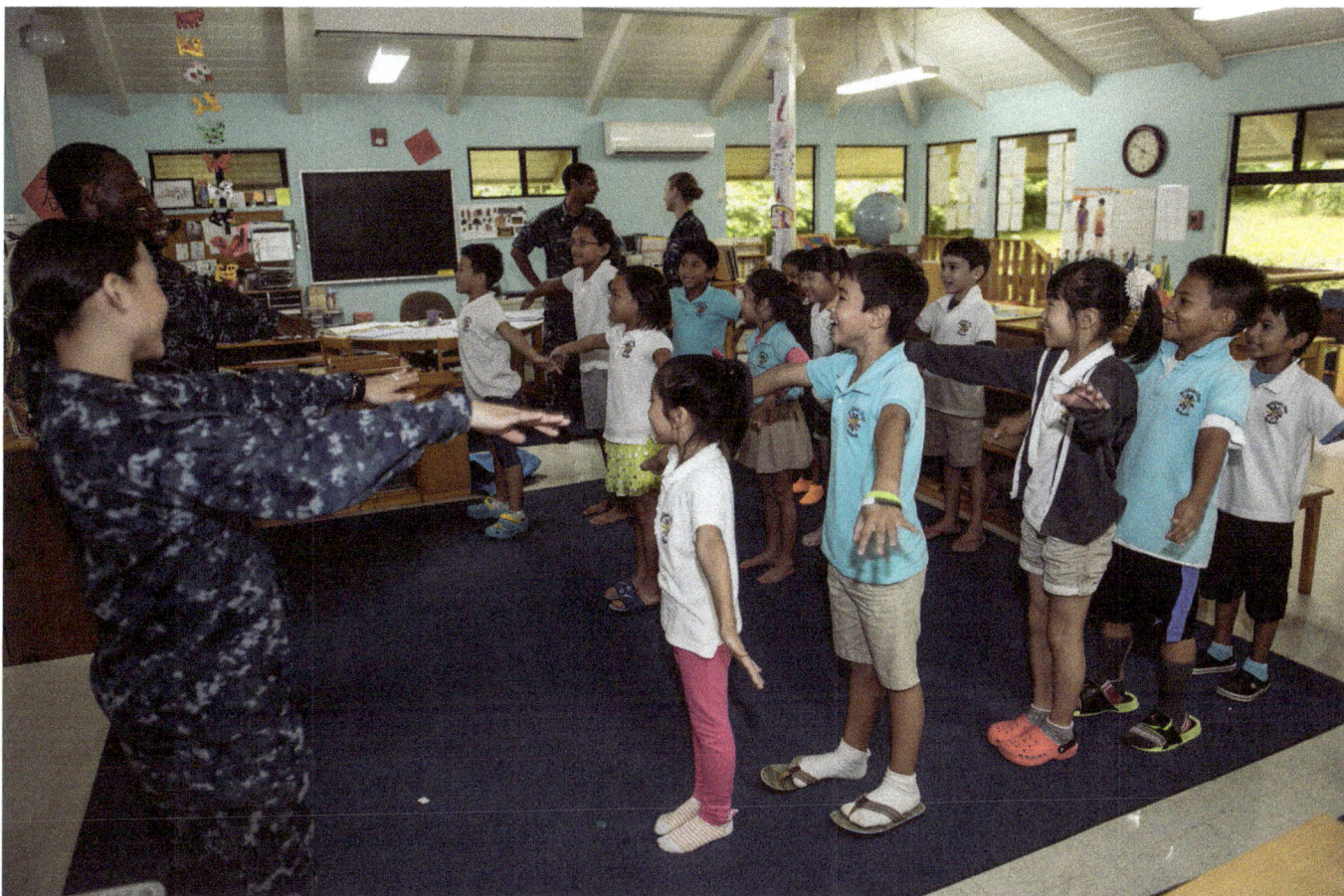

Sailors assigned to the Ticonderoga-class guided-missile cruiser USS Shiloh (CG 67) perform jumping-jacks with students at the Brilliant Star Montessori School in Saipan during a cultural exchange. Shiloh is in Saipan for a scheduled port visit after participating in Valiant Shield, a U.S.-only exercise integrating 18,000 U.S. Navy, Air Force, Army, and Marine Corps personnel, more than 200 aircraft and 19 surface ships, offering real-world joint operational experience to develop capabilities that provide a full range of options to defend U.S. interests and those if its allies and partners. (U.S. Navy photo by Mass Communication Specialist 3rd Class Kevin V. Cunningham/Released)

Chaplain Lt. Autumn M. Wilson, assigned to the Ticonderoga-class guided-missile cruiser USS Shiloh (CG 67), hands out stickers to students at the Brilliant Star Montessori School in Saipan during a cultural exchange. Shiloh is in Saipan for a scheduled port visit after participating in Valiant Shield, a U.S.-only exercise integrating 18,000 U.S. Navy, Air Force, Army, and Marine Corps personnel, more than 200 aircraft and 19 surface ships, offering real-world joint operational experience to develop capabilities that provide a full range of options to defend U.S. interests and those if its allies and partners. (U.S. Navy photo by Mass Communication Specialist 3rd Class Kevin V. Cunningham/Released)

Sailors assigned to the Ticonderoga-class guided-missile cruiser USS Shiloh (CG 67), play games with students at the Brilliant Star Montessori School in Saipan during a cultural exchange. Shiloh is in Saipan for a scheduled port visit after participating in Valiant Shield, a U.S.-only exercise integrating 18,000 U.S. Navy, Air Force, Army, and Marine Corps personnel, more than 200 aircraft and 19 surface ships, offering real-world joint operational experience to develop capabilities that provide a full range of options to defend U.S. interests and those if its allies and partners. (U.S. Navy photo by Mass Communication Specialist 3rd Class Kevin V. Cunningham/Released)

Vice Adm. Thomas Rowden, commander, Naval Surface Forces, U.S. Pacific Fleet, conducts and interview with an Armed Forces Network correspondent during a tour aboard the Ticonderoga-class guided-missile cruiser USS Shiloh (CG 67). Shiloh is assigned to Commander, Task Force 70, and is forward deployed in Yokosuka, Japan, in support of security and stability of the Indo-Asia-Pacific region. (U.S. Navy photo by Fire Controlman First Class Kristopher Horton/Released)

Vice Adm. Thomas Rowden, commander, Naval Surface Forces, U.S. Pacific Fleet, shakes hands with Damage Controlman 2nd Class Luan Nguyen, during a tour onboard the Ticonderoga-class guided-missile cruiser USS Shiloh (CG 67). Shiloh is assigned to Commander, Task Force 70, and is forward deployed in Yokosuka, Japan, in support of security and stability of the Indo-Asia-Pacific region. (U.S. Navy photo by Fire Controlman First Class Kristopher Horton/Released)

Vice Adm. Thomas Rowden, commander, Naval Surface Forces, U.S. Pacific Fleet, talks with Sailors assigned to Ticonderoga-class guided-missile cruiser USS Shiloh (CG 67) during a tour of the ship. Shiloh is assigned to Commander, Task Force 70, and is forward deployed in Yokosuka, Japan, in support of security and stability of the Indo-Asia-Pacific region. (U.S. Navy photo by Fire Controlman First Class Kristopher Horton/Released)

Capt. Kurush F. Morris, right, commanding officer of the Ticonderoga-class guided-missile cruiser USS Shiloh (CG 67), talks with Maj. Gen. Jeffery A. Rockwell, deputy judge advocate, U.S. Air Force, a student from the National Defense University (NDU), during a ship visit. The NDU supports the joint warfighter by providing rigorous joint professional military education to member of the U.S. Armed Forces and select others in order to develop leaders who have the ability to operate and creatively think. Shiloh is assigned to commander, Task Force 70, and is forward deployed to Yokosuka, Japan, to support security and stability of the Indo-Asia-Pacific region. (U.S. Navy photo by Fire Controlman First Class Kristopher Horton/Released)

Capt. Kurush Morris, right, commanding officer of the Ticonderoga-class guided-missile cruiser USS Shiloh (CG 67) talks with members of Japanese media during a ship visit. Shiloh is assigned to Commander, Task Force 70, and is forward deployed to Yokosuka, Japan, to support security and stability of the Indo-Asia-Pacific region. (U.S. Navy photo by Fire Controlman 1st Class Kristopher Horton/Released)

Capt. Kurush Morris, right, commanding officer of the Ticonderoga-class guided-missile cruiser USS Shiloh (CG 67) talks with members of Japanese media during a ship visit. Shiloh is assigned to commander, Task Force 70, and is forward deployed to Yokosuka, Japan, to support security and stability of the Indo-Asia-Pacific region. (U.S. Navy photo by Fire Controlman First Class Kristopher Horton/Released)

A member of Japanese media asks Capt. Kurush Morris, right, commanding officer of the Ticonderoga-class guided-missile cruiser USS Shiloh (CG 67) a question, during a ship visit. Shiloh is assigned to commander, Task Force 70, and is forward deployed to Yokosuka, Japan, to support security and stability of the Indo-Asia-Pacific region. (U.S. Navy photo by Fire Controlman 1st Class Kristopher Horton/Released)

Vice Adm. Robert Thomas, Jr., right, commander, U.S. 7th Fleet shakes hands with Capt. Kurush Morris, left, commanding officer of the Ticonderoga-class guided-missile cruiser USS Shiloh (CG 67), during a ship visit. Shiloh is assigned to commander, Task Force 70, and is forward deployed to Yokosuka, Japan, to support security and stability of the Indo-Asia-Pacific region. (U.S. Navy photo by Fire Controlman First Class Kristopher Horton/Released)

150219-N-N138-107 YOKOSUKA, Japan (Feb. 19, 2015) Rear Adm. Christian Becker, Program Executive Officer (PEO) Command, Control, Communications, Computers and Intelligence (C4I) and PEO Space Systems, talks with Capt. Kurush Morris (left), commanding officer of the Ticonderoga-class guided-missile cruiser USS Shiloh (CG 67), during a ship visit. Shiloh is forward deployed to the 7th Fleet area of operations in support of security and stability in the Indo-Asia-Pacific region. (U.S. Navy photo by Fire Controlman First Class Kristopher Horton/Released)

150219-N-N138-114 YOKOSUKA, Japan (Feb. 19, 2015) Dr. John A. Zangardi (left), Deputy Assistant Secretary of the Navy for Command, Control, Communications, Computers, Intelligence, Information Operations and Space talks with Capt. Kurush Morris, commanding officer of Ticonderoga-class guided-missile cruiser USS Shiloh (CG 67), during a ship visit. Shiloh is forward deployed to the 7th Fleet area of operations in support of security and stability in the Indo-Asia-Pacific region. (U.S. Navy photo by Fire Controlman First Class Kristopher Horton/Released)

150227-N-BB269-023 YOKOSUKA, Japan (Feb. 27, 2015) Capt. Kurush Morris (right), commanding officer of the Ticonderoga-class guided-missile cruiser USS Shiloh (CG 67), explains operations to Japan Self-Defense Force officers during a Fleet Synthetic Training - Joint exercise. Shiloh is forward deployed to Yokosuka, Japan, in support of security and stability in the Indo-Asia Pacific region. (U.S. Navy photo by Mass Communication Specialist 3rd Class Raymond D. Diaz III/Released)

150306-N-LX437-237 WATERS TO THE EAST OF JAPAN (March 6, 2015) Ticonderoga class guided-missile cruiser USS Shiloh (CG 67)'s navigator, Lt. j.g. Crystal Gonzalez (left), conducts training on the ship's bridge with Quartermaster Third Class Samuel Wilson, Boatswain's Mate Seaman Jonny Mejia-Dominguez and Quartermaster Third Class Weston Warr. Shiloh is on patrol in the 7th Fleet area of operation supporting security and stability in the Indo-Asia-Pacific region. (U.S. Navy Photo by Lt. Frederick Martin/Released)

150306-N-LX437-247 *WATERS TO THE EAST OF JAPAN (March 6, 2015) (from left) Quartermasters Third Class Samuel Wilson and Weston Warr, and Boatswain's Mate Seaman Jonny Mejia-Dominguez conduct training on the bridge of Ticonderoga class guided-missile cruiser USS Shiloh (CG 67). Shiloh is on patrol in the 7th Fleet area of operation supporting security and stability in the Indo-Asia-Pacific region. (U.S. Navy Photo by Lt. Frederick Martin/Released)*

150307-N-LX437-013 WATERS TO THE EAST OF JAPAN (March 7, 2015) Gunner's Mate Second Class Keean Durocher conducts pre-fire checks on a .50-caliber M2 machine gun prior to sustainment training on board Ticonderoga class guided-missile cruiser USS Shiloh (CG 67). Shiloh is on patrol in the 7th Fleet area of operation supporting security and stability in the Indo-Asia-Pacific region. (U.S. Navy Photo by Lt. Frederick Martin/Released)

150307-N-LX437-090 *WATERS TO THE EAST OF JAPAN (March 7, 2015) Fire Controlman Second Class Zach Sprouse fires a .50-caliber M2 machine gun during sustainment training on board Ticonderoga class guided-missile cruiser USS Shiloh (CG 67). Shiloh is on patrol in the 7th Fleet area of operation supporting security and stability in the Indo-Asia-Pacific region. (U.S. Navy Photo by Lt. Frederick Martin/Released)*

150310-N-LX437-051 SOUTH CHINA SEA (March 10, 2015) Gas Turbine System Technician (Mechanical) Fireman Bradley Dorn prepares oil samples for inspection in main engine room no. 1 of Ticonderoga class guided-missile cruiser USS Shiloh (CG 67). Shiloh is on patrol in the 7th Fleet area of operation supporting security and stability in the Indo-Asia-Pacific region. (U.S. Navy Photo by Lt. Frederick Martin/Released)

150311-N-LX437-067 SOUTH CHINA SEA (March 11, 2015) Aviation Ordnanceman 2nd Class Scott Burleigh observes Lt. j.g. Scott Collard (center) and Lt. Cmdr. Ryan Campoamor (right) conduct pre-flight checks on an MH-60R assigned to the "Warlords" of Helicopter Maritime Strike squadron (HSM) 51, Det. 4, on board Ticonderoga class guided-missile cruiser USS Shiloh (CG 67). Shiloh is on patrol in the 7th Fleet area of operation supporting security and stability in the Indo-Asia-Pacific region. (U.S. Navy Photo by Lt. Frederick Martin/Released)

150311-N-LX437-124 SOUTH CHINA SEA (March 11, 2015) An MH-60R assigned to the "Warlords" of Helicopter Maritime Strike squadron (HSM) 51, Det. 4, prepares to take off from Ticonderoga class guided-missile cruiser USS Shiloh (CG 67). Shiloh is on patrol in the 7th Fleet area of operation supporting security and stability in the Indo-Asia-Pacific region. (U.S. Navy Photo by Lt. Frederick Martin/Released)

150311-N-LX437-193 SOUTH CHINA SEA (March 11, 2015) Capt. Kurush Morris, commanding officer of Ticonderoga class guided-missile cruiser USS Shiloh (CG 67), speaks with Sailors from Combat Electronics (CE) division in the hangar bay of the ship. CE is the "Division in the Spotlight," a program which rotates focused attention on divisions on board to enhance material, personnel and mission readiness. Shiloh is on patrol in the 7th Fleet area of operation supporting security and stability in the Indo-Asia-Pacific region. (U.S. Navy Photo by Lt. Frederick Martin/Released)

150311-N-LX437-212 SOUTH CHINA SEA (March 11, 2015) Seaman Recruit Zachary Oteney points to the location of a simulated Sailor in the water during a man overboard drill on board Ticonderoga class guided-missile cruiser USS Shiloh (CG 67). Shiloh is on patrol in the 7th Fleet area of operation supporting security and stability in the Indo-Asia-Pacific region. (U.S. Navy Photo by Lt. Frederick Martin/Released)

150311-N-LX437-215 SOUTH CHINA SEA (March 11, 2015) Personnel Specialist Seaman Peyton Irvan (left) and Yeoman 2nd Class William Santiago take muster reports during a man overboard drill on board Ticonderoga class guided-missile cruiser USS Shiloh (CG 67). Shiloh is on patrol in the 7th Fleet area of operation supporting security and stability in the Indo-Asia-Pacific region. (U.S. Navy Photo by Lt. Frederick Martin/Released)

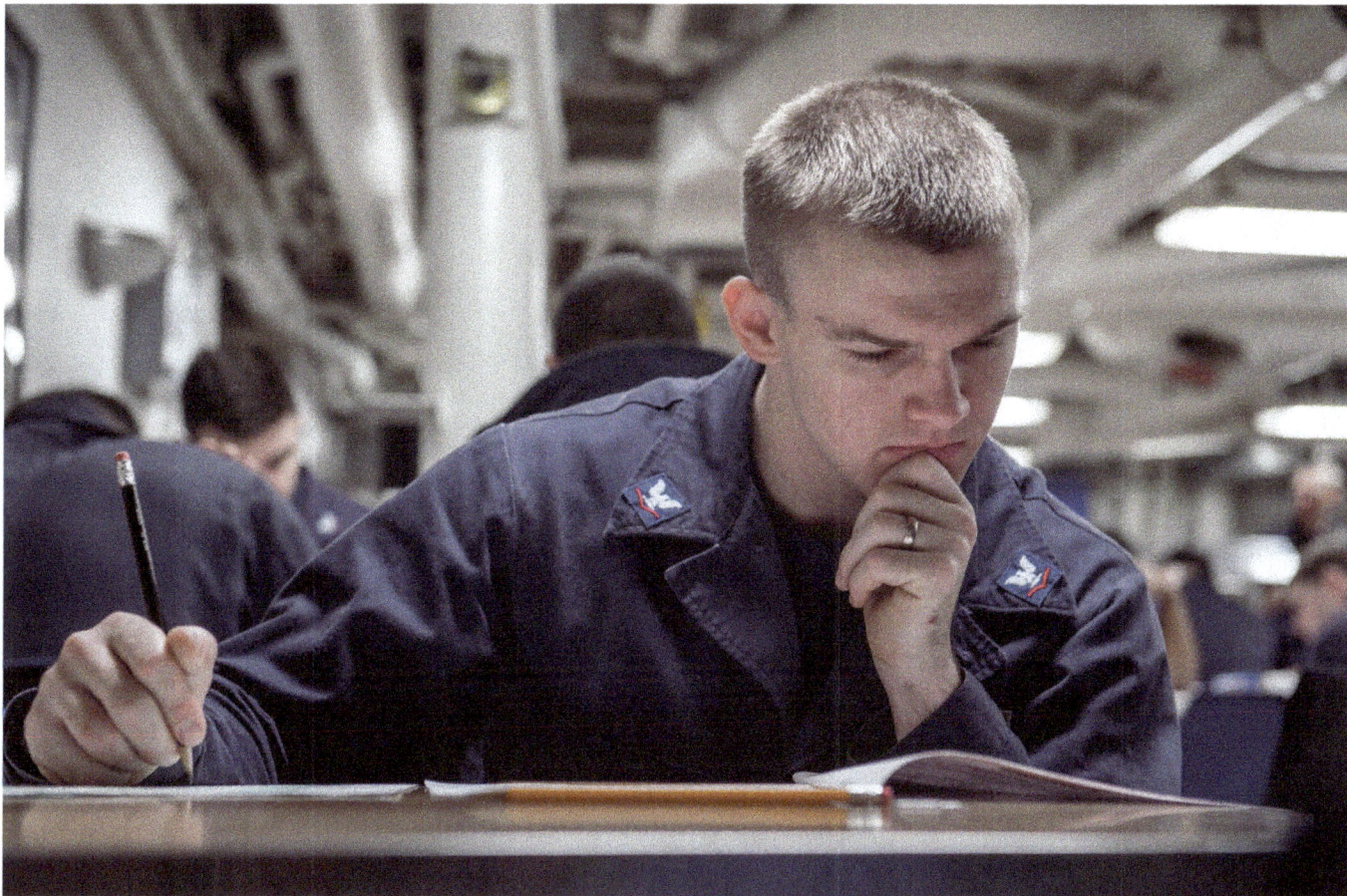

150312-N-LX437-007 SOUTH CHINA SEA (March 12, 2015) Fire Controlman 3rd Class Christopher Wells takes the Navy wide advancement exam on the mess decks of Ticonderoga class guided-missile cruiser USS Shiloh (CG 67). Shiloh is on patrol in the 7th Fleet area of operation supporting security and stability in the Indo-Asia-Pacific region. (U.S. Navy Photo by Lt. Frederick Martin/Released)

150323-N-LX437-114 ADAMAN SEA (March 23, 2015) Ticonderoga class guided-missile cruiser USS Shiloh (CG 67) fires its 5-inch gun during pre-action calibration. Shiloh is on patrol in the 7th Fleet area of operation supporting security and stability in the Indo-Asia-Pacific region. (U.S. Navy Photo by Lt. Frederick Martin/Released)

150323-N-LX437-186 ADAMAN SEA (March 23, 2015) Fire Controlman 2nd Class Robert Ashmore operates the Mk 86 Gun Fire Control System during a pre-action calibration firing of the 5-inch gun on board Ticonderoga class guided-missile cruiser USS Shiloh (CG 67). Shiloh is on patrol in the 7th Fleet area of operation supporting security and stability in the Indo-Asia-Pacific region. (U.S. Navy Photo by Lt. Frederick Martin/Released)

150323-N-LX437-299 ADAMAN SEA (March 23, 2015) Fire Controlman 2nd Class Robert Ashmore operates the Mk 86 Gun Fire Control System during a pre-action calibration firing of the 5-inch gun on board Ticonderoga class guided-missile cruiser USS Shiloh (CG 67). Shiloh is on patrol in the 7th Fleet area of operation supporting security and stability in the Indo-Asia-Pacific region. (U.S. Navy Photo by Lt. Frederick Martin/Released)

150323-N-LX437-383 ADAMAN SEA (March 23, 2015) Gunner's Mate 3rd Class Luis Lozadamarrero uses a bore brush to clean the barrel of a 5-inch gun on board Ticonderoga class guided-missile cruiser USS Shiloh (CG 67). Shiloh is on patrol in the 7th Fleet area of operation supporting security and stability in the Indo-Asia-Pacific region. (U.S. Navy Photo by Lt. Frederick Martin/Released)

150327-N-LX437-115 SINGAPORE (March 27, 2015) Capt. Kurush Morris, commanding officer of Ticonderoga class guided-missile cruiser USS Shiloh (CG 67) speaks to his crew with the 1MC announcing system as the ship pulls into Changi Naval Base in Singapore for a port visit. Shiloh is on patrol in the 7th Fleet area of operation supporting security and stability in the Indo-Asia-Pacific region. (U.S. Navy Photo by Lt. Frederick Martin/Released)

150327-N-LX437-133 SINGAPORE (March 27, 2015) Officers assigned to Ticonderoga class guided-missile cruiser USS Shiloh (CG 67) navigate the ship into Changi Naval Base in Singapore for a port visit. Shiloh is on patrol in the 7th Fleet area of operation supporting security and stability in the Indo-Asia-Pacific region. (U.S. Navy Photo by Lt. Frederick Martin/Released

150327-N-LX437-159 SINGAPORE (March 27, 2015) Quartermaster 3rd Class Weston Warr (right) plots navigational fixes while Operations Specialist 3rd Class Chelsee Champagne relays navigational information from the Combat Information Center on board Ticonderoga class guided-missile cruiser USS Shiloh (CG 67) as the ship pulls into Changi Naval Base in Singapore for a port visit. Shiloh is on patrol in the 7th Fleet area of operation supporting security and stability in the Indo-Asia-Pacific region. (U.S. Navy Photo by Lt. Frederick Martin/Released)

150327-N-LX437-196 SINGAPORE (March 27, 2015) Sailors haul in a line from a tug as the Ticonderoga class guided-missile cruiser USS Shiloh (CG 67) pulls into Changi Naval Base in Singapore for a port visit. Shiloh is on patrol in the 7th Fleet area of operation supporting security and stability in the Indo-Asia-Pacific region. (U.S. Navy Photo by Lt. Frederick Martin/Released)

150401-N-LX437-136 SOUTH CHINA SEA (April 1, 2015) Boatswain's Mate Seaman Apprentice Robert Yawn mans a smoke boundary during a fire drill on board Ticonderoga class guided-missile cruiser USS Shiloh (CG 67). Shiloh is on patrol in the 7th Fleet area of operation supporting security and stability in the Indo-Asia-Pacific region. (U.S. Navy Photo by Lt. Frederick Martin/Released)

150401-N-LX437-142 SOUTH CHINA SEA (April 1, 2015) Sailors from a fire team of Ticonderoga class guided-missile cruiser USS Shiloh (CG 67) enter a smoke-filled space during a fire drill on board the ship. Shiloh is on patrol in the 7th Fleet area of operation supporting security and stability in the Indo-Asia-Pacific region. (U.S. Navy Photo by Lt. Frederick Martin/Released)

150401-N-LX437-383 SOUTH CHINA SEA (April 1, 2015) Electronics Technician 3rd Class Christian Windsor (right) fires a .50-caliber machine gun under the supervision of line coach Gunner's Mate 2nd Class Keean Durocher during a qualification course on board Ticonderoga class guided-missile cruiser USS Shiloh (CG 67). Shiloh is on patrol in the 7th Fleet area of operation supporting security and stability in the Indo-Asia-Pacific region. (U.S. Navy Photo by Lt. Frederick Martin/Released)

150401-N-LX437-479 SOUTH CHINA SEA (April 1, 2015) *Boatswain's Mate Seaman Caleb Cloud (right) fires a .50-caliber machine gun under the supervision of line coach Gunner's Mate 2nd Class Keean Durocher during a qualification course on board Ticonderoga class guided-missile cruiser USS Shiloh (CG 67). Shiloh is on patrol in the 7th Fleet area of operation supporting security and stability in the Indo-Asia-Pacific region. (U.S. Navy Photo by Lt. Frederick Martin/Released)*

150412-N-LX437-028 ADAMAN SEA (April 12, 2015) Naval Aircrewman Tactical Helicopter 2nd Class Kevin Lawson conducts a pre-flight check on the rescue hoist of an MH-60R Seahawk assigned to Helicopter Maritime Strike Squadron (HSM) 51 "Warlords," Det. 4 prior to take off from Ticonderoga class guided-missile cruiser USS Shiloh (CG 67). Shiloh is on patrol in the 7th Fleet area of operation supporting security and stability in the Indo-Asia-Pacific region. (U.S. Navy Photo by Lt. Frederick Martin/Released)

150412-N-LX437-108 ADAMAN SEA (April 12, 2015) *Boatswain's Mate Seaman Joshua Buell (right) indicates the position of Sailors as they remove chocks and chains from an MH-60R Seahawk assigned to Helicopter Maritime Strike Squadron (HSM) 51 "Warlords," Det. 4 prior to take off from Ticonderoga class guided-missile cruiser USS Shiloh (CG 67). Shiloh is on patrol in the 7th Fleet area of operation supporting security and stability in the Indo-Asia-Pacific region. (U.S. Navy Photo by Lt. Frederick Martin/Released)*

150412-N-LX437-220 ADAMAN SEA (April 12, 2015) An MH-60R Seahawk assigned to Helicopter Maritime Strike Squadron (HSM) 51 "Warlords," Det. 4 takes off from Ticonderoga class guided-missile cruiser USS Shiloh (CG 67). Shiloh is on patrol in the 7th Fleet area of operation supporting security and stability in the Indo-Asia-Pacific region. (U.S. Navy Photo by Lt. Frederick Martin/Released)

150412-N-LX437-291 ADAMAN SEA (April 12, 2015) Lt. Joseph Baker operates the Landing Signals Officer (LSO) control panel during the launch of an MH-60R Seahawk assigned to Helicopter Maritime Strike Squadron (HSM) 51 "Warlords," Det. 4 from Ticonderoga class guided-missile cruiser USS Shiloh (CG 67). Shiloh is on patrol in the 7th Fleet area of operation supporting security and stability in the Indo-Asia-Pacific region. (U.S. Navy Photo by Lt. Frederick Martin/Released)

150422-N-LX437-134 PHILIPPINE SEA (April 22, 2015) Ticonderoga class guided-missile cruiser USS Shiloh (CG 67) fires its 5-inch gun during pre-action calibration drill. Shiloh is on patrol in the 7th Fleet area of operation supporting security and stability in the Indo-Asia-Pacific region. (U.S. Navy Photo by Lt. Frederick Martin/Released)

150422-N-LX437-228 PHILIPPINE SEA (April 22, 2015) Ticonderoga class guided-missile cruiser USS Shiloh (CG 67) fires its 5-inch gun during pre-action calibration drill. Shiloh is on patrol in the 7th Fleet area of operation supporting security and stability in the Indo-Asia-Pacific region. (U.S. Navy Photo by Lt. Frederick Martin/Released)

150604-N-BB269-010 PHILIPPINE SEA (June 4, 2015) Quarter Master 2nd Class Weston Warr, from Salt Lake City, assigned to the Ticonderoga-class guided-missile cruiser USS Shiloh (CG 67), hoists down the ship's restrictive maneuvering day shapes after flight quarters. Shiloh is on patrol in the U.S. 7th Fleet area of responsibility in support of security and stability in the Indo-Asia Pacific region. (U.S. Navy photo by Mass Communication Specialist 2nd Class Raymond D. Diaz III/Released)

150604-N-BB269-027 PHILIPPINE SEA (June 4, 2015) The Ticonderoga-class guided-missile cruiser USS Shiloh (CG 67) fires her Phalanx close-in weapons system (CIWS) during a live-fire exercise. Shiloh is on patrol in the U.S. 7th Fleet area of responsibility in support of security and stability in the Indo-Asia Pacific region. (U.S. Navy photo by Mass Communication Specialist 2nd Class Raymond D. Diaz III/Released)

150605-N-BB269-086 PHILIPPINE SEA (June 5, 2015) The Ticonderoga-class guided-missile cruiser USS Shiloh (CG 67) fires her MK 45 5-inch gun during a live-fire gunnery exercise. Shiloh is on patrol in the U.S. 7th Fleet area of responsibility in support of security and stability in the Indo-Asia Pacific region. (U.S. Navy photo by Mass Communication Specialist 2nd Class Raymond D. Diaz III/Released)

150611-N-BB269-011 APRA HARBOR, Guam (June 11, 2015) The Ticonderoga-class guided-missile cruiser USS Shiloh (CG 67) transits into Apra Harbor, for a port visit. Shiloh is on patrol in the U.S. 7th Fleet area of responsibility in support of security and stability in the Indo-Asia Pacific region. (U.S. Navy photo by Mass Communication Specialist 2nd Class Raymond D. Diaz III/Released)

150611-N-BB269-085 APRA HARBOR, Guam (June 11, 2015) Lt. Chad McCain (top), a Navy chaplain, and Quartermaster Seaman Alexis Walker, both assigned to the Ticonderoga-class guided-missile cruiser USS Shiloh (CG 67), fold the national ensign after the ship moors at Apra Harbor, for a port visit. Shiloh is on patrol in the U.S. 7th Fleet area of responsibility in support of security and stability in the Indo-Asia Pacific region. (U.S. Navy photo by Mass Communication Specialist 2nd Class Raymond D. Diaz III/Released)

191207-N-OI558-2042 SASEBO, Japan (Dec. 7, 2019) Capt. Sharif Calfee, oncoming commanding officer of the USS Shiloh, introduces himself to the crew during a change of command ceremony aboard the Ticonderoga-class guided-missile cruiser USS Shiloh (CG 67). Shiloh is forward-deployed to the U.S. 7th Fleet area of operations in support of security and stability in the Indo-Pacific region. (U.S. Navy photo by Mass Communication Specialist 3rd Class Chanel L. Turner)

191207-N-OI558-2049 SASEBO, Japan (Dec. 7, 2019) Capt. Sharif Calfee, oncoming commanding officer of the USS Shiloh, shake hands Capt. Robert "Bo" Johns, off-going commanding officer of the USS Shiloh during a change of command ceremony aboard the Ticonderoga-class guided-missile cruiser USS Shiloh (CG 67). Shiloh is forward-deployed to the U.S. 7th Fleet area of operations in support of security and stability in the Indo-Pacific region. (U.S. Navy photo by Mass Communication Specialist 3rd Class Chanel L. Turner)

191207-N-OI558-2212 SASEBO, Japan (Dec. 7, 2019) Capt. Sharif Calfee, oncoming commanding officer of the USS Shiloh, introduces himself to the crew during a change of command ceremony aboard the Ticonderoga-class guided-missile cruiser USS Shiloh (CG 67). Shiloh is forward-deployed to the U.S. 7th Fleet area of operations in support of security and stability in the Indo-Pacific region. (U.S. Navy photo by Mass Communication Specialist 3rd Class Chanel L. Turner)

191207-N-OI558-2220 SASEBO, Japan (Dec. 7, 2019) Capt. Sharif Calfee, oncoming commanding officer of the USS Shiloh, introduces himself to the crew during a change of command ceremony aboard the Ticonderoga-class guided-missile cruiser USS Shiloh (CG 67). Shiloh is forward-deployed to the U.S. 7th Fleet area of operations in support of security and stability in the Indo-Pacific region. (U.S. Navy photo by Mass Communication Specialist 3rd Class Chanel L. Turner)

191207-N-OI558-2233 SASEBO, Japan (Dec. 7, 2019) Capt. Sharif Calfee, oncoming commanding officer of the USS Shiloh, introduces himself to the crew during a change of command ceremony aboard the Ticonderoga-class guided-missile cruiser USS Shiloh (CG 67). Shiloh is forward-deployed to the U.S. 7th Fleet area of operations in support of security and stability in the Indo-Pacific region. (U.S. Navy photo by Mass Communication Specialist 3rd Class Chanel L. Turner)

191218-N-OI558-1279 SOUTH CHINA SEA (Dec. 18, 2019) Gunner's Mate Seaman Jonathan Winfield (left) and Boatswain's Mate 2nd Class Joseph Panganiban attach cargo to an MH-60R Sea Hawk helicopter assigned to the "Warlords" of Helicopter Maritime Strike Squadron (HSM) 51 during replenishment-at-sea aboard aboard the Ticonderoga-class guided missile cruiser USS Shiloh (CG 67). Shiloh is forward-deployed to the U.S. 7th Fleet area of operations in support of security and stability in the Indo-Pacific region. (U.S. Navy photo by Mass Communication Specialist 3rd Class Chanel L. Turner)

191218-N-OI558-1403 SOUTH CHINA SEA (Dec. 18, 2019) Boatswain's Mate 3rd Class Justin Walker signals an MH-60R Sea Hawk helicopter assigned to the "Warlords" of Helicopter Maritime Strike Squadron (HSM) 51 during replenishment-at-sea aboard aboard the Ticonderoga-class guided missile cruiser USS Shiloh (CG 67). Shiloh is forward-deployed to the U.S. 7th Fleet area of operations in support of security and stability in the Indo-Pacific region. (U.S. Navy photo by Mass Communication Specialist 3rd Class Chanel L. Turner)

191219-N-OI558-1075 SOUTH CHINA SEA (Dec. 19, 2019) Machinist Mate 2nd Class Matthew Dibblee performs maintenance aboard the Ticonderoga-class guided missile cruiser USS Shiloh (CG 67). Shiloh is forward-deployed to the U.S. 7th Fleet area of operations in support of security and stability in the Indo-Pacific region. (U.S. Navy photo by Mass Communication Specialist 3rd Class Chanel L. Turner)

191220-N-OI558-1159 SOUTH CHINA SEA (Dec. 20, 2019) Ensign Henry Palmer participates in a surface security drill aboard the Ticonderoga-class guided missile cruiser USS Shiloh (CG 67). Shiloh is forward-deployed to the U.S. 7th Fleet area of operations in support of security and stability in the Indo-Pacific region. (U.S. Navy photo by Mass Communication Specialist 3rd Class Chanel L. Turner)

191220-N-OI558-1246 SOUTH CHINA SEA (Dec. 20, 2019) Operations Specialist 1st Class Ellington Morgan trains Sailors in a surface security drill aboard the Ticonderoga-class guided missile cruiser USS Shiloh (CG 67). Shiloh is forward-deployed to the U.S. 7th Fleet area of operations in support of security and stability in the Indo-Pacific region. (U.S. Navy photo by Mass Communication Specialist 3rd Class Chanel L. Turner)

191220-N-OI558-1290 SOUTH CHINA SEA (Dec. 20, 2019) Fire Controlman (Ageis) 2nd Class Jonathan Okoro in a surface security drill aboard the Ticonderoga-class guided missile cruiser USS Shiloh (CG 67). Shiloh is forward-deployed to the U.S. 7th Fleet area of operations in support of security and stability in the Indo-Pacific region. (U.S. Navy photo by Mass Communication Specialist 3rd Class Chanel L. Turner)

191221-N-OI558-1006 SOUTH CHINA SEA (Dec. 21, 2019) Sailors aboard Ticonderoga-class guided-missile cruiser USS Shiloh (CG 67) conducts a replenishment-at-sea with the fleet replenishment ship USNS John Erickson (T-AO 194) USNS John Erikson. Shiloh is forward-deployed to the U.S. 7th Fleet area of operations in support of security and stability in the Indo-Pacific region. (U.S. Navy photo by Mass Communication Specialist 3rd Class Chanel L. Turner)

191221-N-OI558-1098 SOUTH CHINA SEA (Dec. 21, 2019) The aboard Ticonderoga-class guided-missile cruiser USS Shiloh (CG 67) conducts a replenishment-at-sea with the fleet replenishment ship USNS John Erickson (T-AO 194) USNS John Erikson. Shiloh is forward-deployed to the U.S. 7th Fleet area of operations in support of security and stability in the Indo-Pacific region. (U.S. Navy photo by Mass Communication Specialist 3rd Class Chanel L. Turner)

191221-N-OI558-1121 SOUTH CHINA SEA (Dec. 21, 2019) The aboard Ticonderoga-class guided-missile cruiser USS Shiloh (CG 67) conducts a replenishment-at-sea with the fleet replenishment ship USNS John Erickson (T-AO 194) USNS John Erikson. Shiloh is forward-deployed to the U.S. 7th Fleet area of operations in support of security and stability in the Indo-Pacific region. (U.S. Navy photo by Mass Communication Specialist 3rd Class Chanel L. Turner)

190104-N-OI558-1165 SOUTH CHINA SEA (Jan. 4, 2019) Retail Specialist Seaman Matthew R. Powell adjusts his self-contained breathing apparatus while participating in a damage control drill aboard the Ticonderoga-class guided missile cruiser USS Shiloh (CG 67). Shiloh is forward-deployed to the U.S. 7th Fleet area of operations in support of security and stability in the Indo-Pacific region. (U.S. Navy photo by Mass Communication Specialist 3rd Class Chanel L. Turner)

190104-N-OI558-1243 SOUTH CHINA SEA (Jan. 4, 2019) Damage Controlman 1st

Class Marivic D. Abad instructs Sailors during a damage control drill aboard the Ticonderoga-class guided missile cruiser USS Shiloh (CG 67). Shiloh is forward-deployed to the U.S. 7th Fleet area of operations in support of security and stability in the Indo-Pacific region. (U.S. Navy photo by Mass Communication Specialist 3rd Class Chanel L. Turner)

190104-N-OI558-1327 SOUTH CHINA SEA (Jan. 4, 2019) Lt. j.g Greg Hudik, from Yelm, Wash., mark charts during a damage control drill aboard the Ticonderoga-class guided missile cruiser USS Shiloh (CG 67). Shiloh is forward-deployed to the U.S. 7th Fleet area of operations in support of security and stability in the Indo-Pacific region. (U.S. Navy photo by Mass Communication Specialist 3rd Class Chanel L. Turner)

190104-N-OI558-1327 *SOUTH CHINA SEA (Jan. 4, 2019) Ensign Luke Lanham, from South Lake, Texas, participates in a damage control drill aboard the Ticonderoga-class guided missile cruiser USS Shiloh (CG 67). Shiloh is forward-deployed to the U.S. 7th Fleet area of operations in support of security and stability in the Indo-Pacific region. (U.S. Navy photo by Mass Communication Specialist 3rd Class Chanel L. Turner)*

190104-N-OI558-1565 SOUTH CHINA SEA (Jan. 4, 2019) Sailors put out a simulated fire during a damage control drill aboard the Ticonderoga-class guided missile cruiser USS Shiloh (CG 67). Shiloh is forward-deployed to the U.S. 7th Fleet area of operations in support of security and stability in the Indo-Pacific region. (U.S. Navy photo by Mass Communication Specialist 3rd Class Chanel L. Turner)

190104-N-OI558-1138 SOUTH CHINA SEA (Jan. 4, 2019) Retail Specialist Matthew R. Powell adjusts his self-contained breathing apparatus while participating in a damage control drill aboard the Ticonderoga-class guided missile cruiser USS Shiloh (CG 67). Shiloh is forward-deployed to the U.S. 7th Fleet area of operations in support of security and stability in the Indo-Pacific region. (U.S. Navy photo by Mass Communication Specialist 3rd Class Chanel L. Turner)

190104-N-OI558-1197 SOUTH CHINA SEA (Jan. 4, 2019) Yeoman Class 2nd Dylan G. Zuker participates in a damage control drill aboard the Ticonderoga-class guided missile cruiser USS Shiloh (CG 67). Shiloh is forward-deployed to the U.S. 7th Fleet area of operations in support of security and stability in the Indo-Pacific region. (U.S. Navy photo by Mass Communication Specialist 3rd Class Chanel L. Turner)

190104-N-OI558-1261 SOUTH CHINA SEA (Jan. 4, 2019) Retail Specialist 2nd Class Edward P. Dingle inspects spaces during a damage control drill aboard the Ticonderoga-class guided missile cruiser USS Shiloh (CG 67). Shiloh is forward-deployed to the U.S. 7th Fleet area of operations in support of security and stability in the Indo-Pacific region. (U.S. Navy photo by Mass Communication Specialist 3rd Class Chanel L. Turner)

190104-N-OI558-1279 SOUTH CHINA SEA (Jan. 4, 2019) Retail Specialist 2nd Class Edward P. Dingle climbs out a hatch during a damage control drill aboard the Ticonderoga-class guided missile cruiser USS Shiloh (CG 67). Shiloh is forward-deployed to the U.S. 7th Fleet area of operations in support of security and stability in the Indo-Pacific region. (U.S. Navy photo by Mass Communication Specialist 3rd Class Chanel L. Turner)

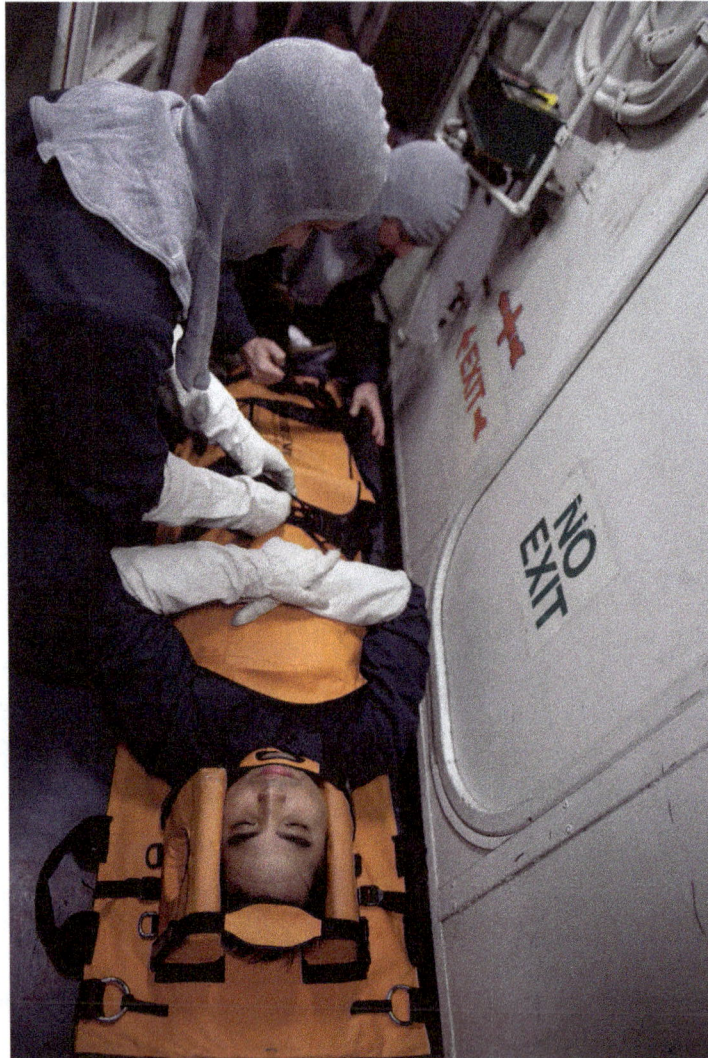

190104-N-OI558-1011 SOUTH CHINA SEA (Jan. 4, 2019) Boatswain's Mate 2nd Class Joseph C. Panganiban simulates an injury while participating in a damage control drill aboard the Ticonderoga-class guided missile cruiser USS Shiloh (CG 67). Shiloh is forward-deployed to the U.S. 7th Fleet area of operations in support of security and stability in the Indo-Pacific region. (U.S. Navy photo by Mass Communication Specialist 3rd Class Chanel L. Turner)

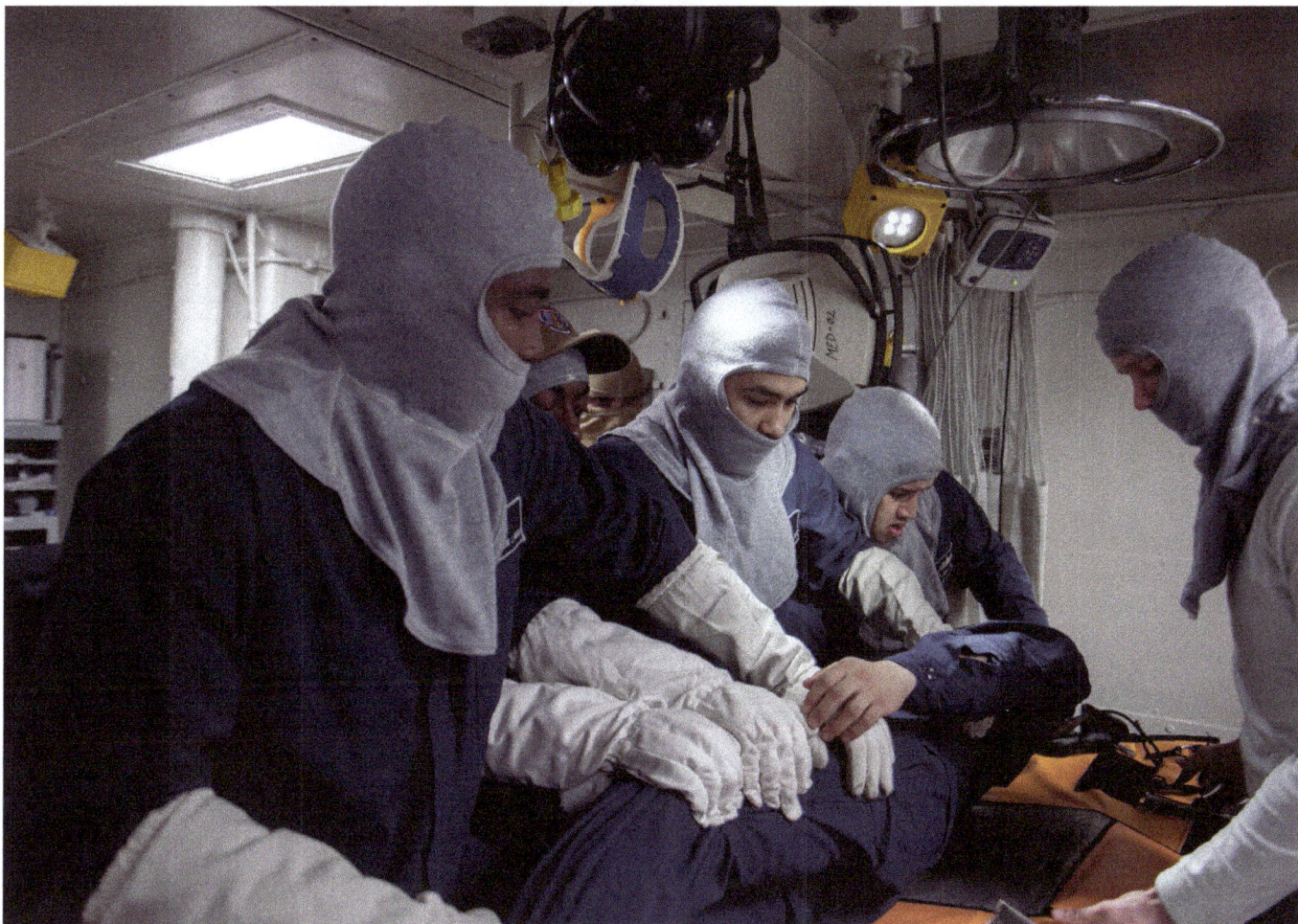

190104-N-OI558-1075 SOUTH CHINA SEA (Jan. 4, 2019) Sailors turnover a simulated injury patient while participating in a damage control drill aboard the Ticonderoga-class guided missile cruiser USS Shiloh (CG 67). Shiloh is forward-deployed to the U.S. 7th Fleet area of operations in support of security and stability in the Indo-Pacific region. (U.S. Navy photo by Mass Communication Specialist 3rd Class Chanel L. Turner)

190106-N-OI558-1027 SOUTH CHINA SEA (Jan. 6, 2019) Logistics Specialist 2nd Class Prycilla N. Saldivar practices chest compressions during an CPR training aboard the Ticonderoga-class guided missile cruiser USS Shiloh (CG 67). Shiloh is forward-deployed to the U.S. 7th Fleet area of operations in support of security and stability in the Indo-Pacific region. (U.S. Navy photo by Mass Communication Specialist 3rd Class Chanel L. Turner)

190106-N-OI558-1063 SOUTH CHINA SEA (Jan. 6, 2019) Cryptologic Technician (Collection) 2nd Class Kyle Druilhet practices chest compressions during a CPR training aboard the Ticonderoga-class guided missile cruiser USS Shiloh (CG 67). Shiloh is forward-deployed to the U.S. 7th Fleet area of operations in support of security and stability in the Indo-Pacific region. (U.S. Navy photo by Mass Communication Specialist 3rd Class Chanel L. Turner)

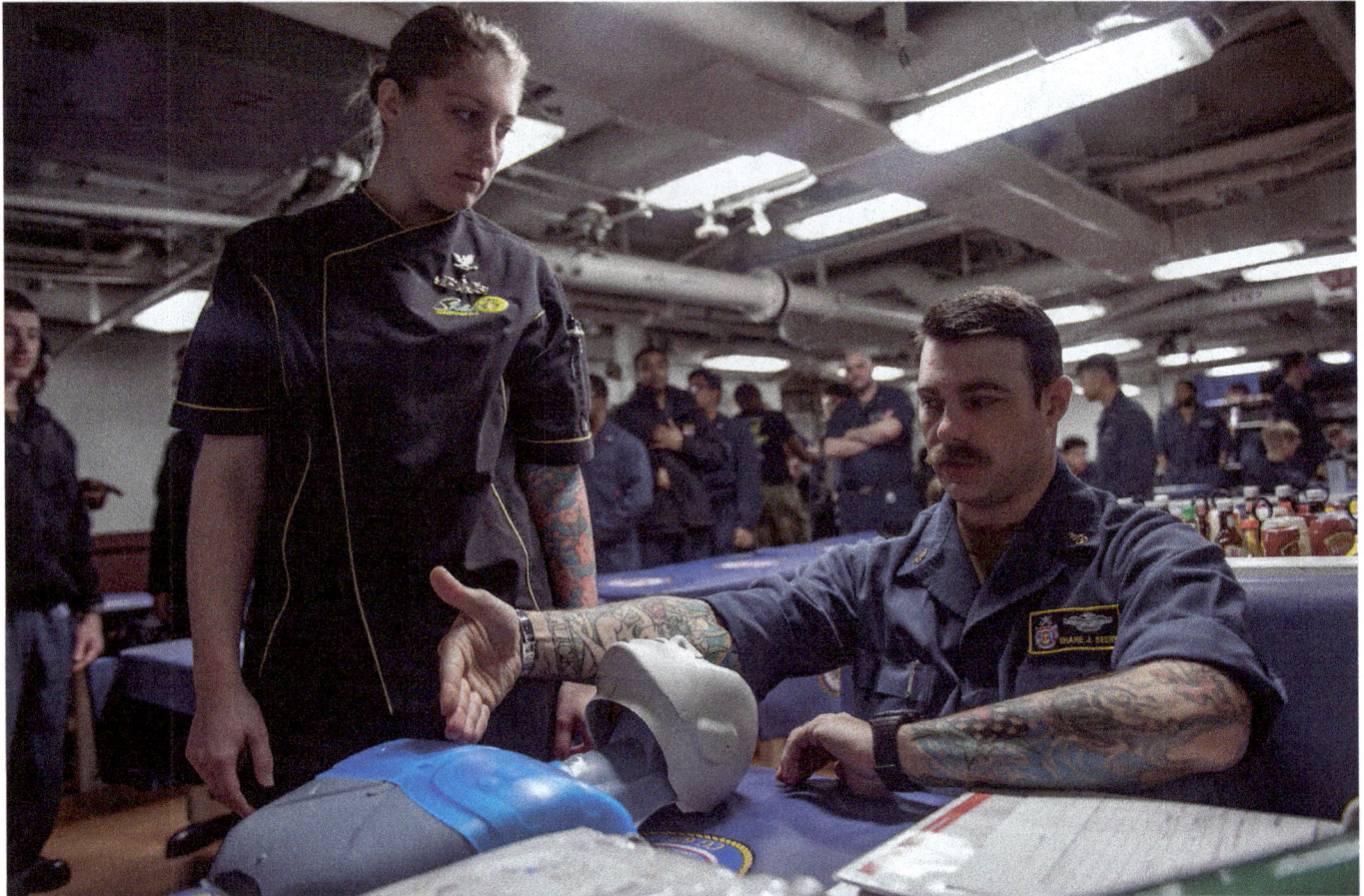

190106-N-OI558-1063 SOUTH CHINA SEA (Jan. 6, 2019) Senior Chief Hospital Corpsman Shane J. Seery, teaches chest compressions during CPR training aboard the Ticonderoga-class guided missile cruiser USS Shiloh (CG 67). Shiloh is forward-deployed to the U.S. 7th Fleet area of operations in support of security and stability in the Indo-Pacific region. (U.S. Navy photo by Mass Communication Specialist 3rd Class Chanel L. Turner)

200113-N-OI558-1038 EAST CHINA SEA (Jan. 13, 2019) Fire Controlman 2nd Class Christopher S. Albritton shoots an M-14 rifle during a replenishment-at-sea aboard the Ticonderoga-class guided missile cruiser USS Shiloh (CG 67). Shiloh is forward-deployed to the U.S. 7th Fleet area of operations in support of security and stability in the Indo-Pacific region. (U.S. Navy photo by Mass Communication Specialist 3rd Class Chanel L. Turner)

200113-N-OI558-1075 *EAST CHINA SEA (Jan. 13, 2019) Electronics Technician 2nd Class Vincent D. McCall tightens up a line during a replenishment-at-sea aboard the Ticonderoga-class guided missile cruiser USS Shiloh (CG 67). Shiloh is forward-deployed to the U.S. 7th Fleet area of operations in support of security and stability in the Indo-Pacific region. (U.S. Navy photo by Mass Communication Specialist 3rd Class Chanel L. Turner)*

200113-N-OI558-1234 EAST CHINA SEA (Jan. 13, 2019) *Sailors heave a phone and distance line during a replenishment-at-sea aboard the Ticonderoga-class guided missile cruiser USS Shiloh (CG 67). Shiloh is forward-deployed to the U.S. 7th Fleet area of operations in support of security and stability in the Indo-Pacific region. (U.S. Navy photo by Mass Communication Specialist 3rd Class Chanel L. Turner)*

200113-N-OI558-1614 EAST CHINA SEA (Jan. 13, 2019) Sailors move supplies on the mess decks of the Ticonderoga-class guided missile cruiser USS Shiloh (CG 67) during a replenishment-at-sea. Shiloh is forward-deployed to the U.S. 7th Fleet area of operations in support of security and stability in the Indo-Pacific region. (U.S. Navy photo by Mass Communication Specialist 3rd Class Chanel L. Turner)

200115-N-OI558-1009 PHILLIPINES SEA (Jan. 15, 2019) Seaman Nicholas Lioy, left, and Seaman Scott Rapp set up bullets during a .50-caliber machine gun shoot aboard the Ticonderoga-class guided missile cruiser USS Shiloh (CG 67). Shiloh is forward-deployed to the U.S. 7th Fleet area of operations in support of security and stability in the Indo-Pacific region. (U.S. Navy photo by Mass Communication Specialist 3rd Class Chanel L. Turner)

200115-N-OI558-1115 PHILLIPINES SEA (Jan. 15, 2019) Sailors conduct a 50-caliber machine gun shoot aboard the Ticonderoga-class guided missile cruiser USS Shiloh (CG 67). Shiloh is forward-deployed to the U.S. 7th Fleet area of operations in support of security and stability in the Indo-Pacific region. (U.S. Navy photo by Mass Communication Specialist 3rd Class Chanel L. Turner)

200119-N-OI558-1080 EAST CHINA SEA (Jan. 19, 2020) Quartermaster Seaman Meghan B. Stephens, left, simulates an injury while participating in a damage control drill aboard the Ticonderoga-class guided missile cruiser USS Shiloh (CG 67). Shiloh is forward-deployed to the U.S. 7th Fleet area of operations in support of security and stability in the Indo-Pacific region. (U.S. Navy photo by Mass Communication Specialist 3rd Class Chanel L. Turner)

200119-N-OI558-1173 *EAST CHINA SEA (Jan. 19, 2020) Sailors simulate flooding repair while participating in a damage control drill aboard the Ticonderoga-class guided missile cruiser USS Shiloh (CG 67). Shiloh is forward-deployed to the U.S. 7th Fleet area of operations in support of security and stability in the Indo-Pacific region. (U.S. Navy photo by Mass Communication Specialist 3rd Class Chanel L. Turner)*

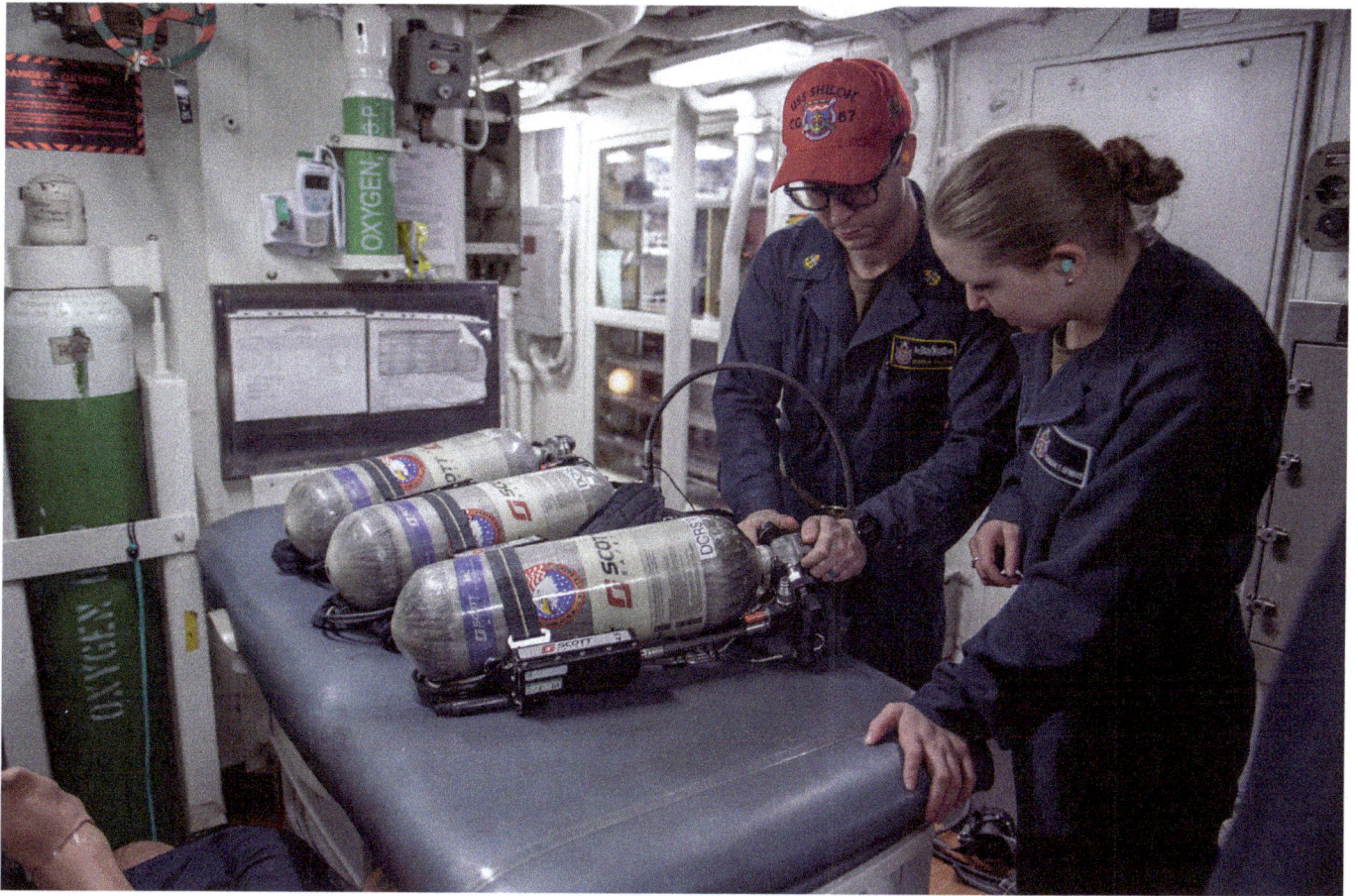

200119-N-OI558-1236 EAST CHINA SEA (Jan. 19, 2020) Chief Damage Controlman Brandon E. Gregrow, left, trains Fireman Savannah F. Hennecy on self-contained breathing apparatuses while participating in a damage control drill aboard the Ticonderoga-class guided missile cruiser USS Shiloh (CG 67). Shiloh is forward-deployed to the U.S. 7th Fleet area of operations in support of security and stability in the Indo-Pacific region. (U.S. Navy photo by Mass Communication Specialist 3rd Class Chanel L. Turner)

200120-N-OI558-1157 *EAST CHINA SEA (Jan. 20, 2020) Boatswain's Mate 3rd Class Justin A. Walker signals an MH-60R Sea Hawk helicopter assigned to the "Warlords" of Helicopter Maritime Strike Squadron (HSM) 51 during a vertical replenishment aboard the Ticonderoga-class guided missile cruiser USS Shiloh (CG 67). Shiloh is forward-deployed to the U.S. 7th Fleet area of operations in support of security and stability in the Indo-Pacific region. (U.S. Navy photo by Mass Communication Specialist 3rd Class Chanel L. Turner)*

200120-N-OI558-1253 EAST CHINA SEA (Jan. 20, 2020) Boatswain's Mate 3rd Class Justin A. Walker signals an MH-60R Sea Hawk helicopter assigned to the "Warlords" of Helicopter Maritime Strike Squadron (HSM) 51 during a vertical replenishment aboard the Ticonderoga-class guided missile cruiser USS Shiloh (CG 67). Shiloh is forward-deployed to the U.S. 7th Fleet area of operations in support of security and stability in the Indo-Pacific region. (U.S. Navy photo by Mass Communication Specialist 3rd Class Chanel L. Turner)

200121-N-OI558-1150 EAST CHINA SEA (Jan. 21, 2020) An MH-60R Sea Hawk helicopter assigned to the "Warlords" of Helicopter Maritime Strike Squadron (HSM) 51 conducts a vertical replenishment with the Ticonderoga-class guided missile cruiser USS Shiloh (CG 67). Shiloh is forward-deployed to the U.S. 7th Fleet area of operations in support of security and stability in the Indo-Pacific region. (U.S. Navy photo by Mass Communication Specialist 3rd Class Chanel L. Turner)

200121-N-OI558-1160 EAST CHINA SEA (Jan. 21, 2020) An MH-60R Sea Hawk helicopter assigned to the "Warlords" of Helicopter Maritime Strike Squadron (HSM) 51 conducts a vertical replenishment with the Ticonderoga-class guided missile cruiser USS Shiloh (CG 67). Shiloh is forward-deployed to the U.S. 7th Fleet area of operations in support of security and stability in the Indo-Pacific region. (U.S. Navy photo by Mass Communication Specialist 3rd Class Chanel L. Turner)

200308-N-KW492-0206 PHILIPPINE SEA (Mar. 8, 2020) Sailors assigned to the Ticonderoga-class guided-missile cruiser USS Shiloh (CG 67) approach a life raft on a rigid-hull inflatable boat during small boat operations. Shiloh is forward-deployed to the U.S. 7th Fleet area of operations in support of security and stability in the Indo-Pacific region. (U.S. Navy photo by Mass Communication Specialist 2nd Class Ryre Arciaga)

200308-N-KW492-0325 PHILIPPINE SEA (Mar. 8, 2020) Sailors on a rigid-hull inflatable boat assigned to the Ticonderoga-class guided-missile cruiser USS Shiloh (CG 67) investigate a life raft while conducting small boat operations. Shiloh is forward-deployed to the U.S. 7th Fleet area of operations in support of security and stability in the Indo-Pacific region. (U.S. Navy photo by Mass Communication Specialist 2nd Class Ryre Arciaga)

200308-N-KW492-0425 PHILIPPINE SEA (Mar. 8, 2020) Sailors assigned to the Ticonderoga-class guided-missile cruiser USS Shiloh (CG 67) operate a rigid-hull inflatable boat while conducting small boat operations. Shiloh is forward-deployed to the U.S. 7th Fleet area of operations in support of security and stability in the Indo-Pacific region. (U.S. Navy photo by Mass Communication Specialist 2nd Class Ryre Arciaga)

200309-N-KW492-0082 PHILIPPINE SEA (Mar. 9, 2020) Sailors salute the Ticonderoga-class guided-missile cruiser USS Antietam (CG 54) aboard the fantail of the Ticonderoga-class guided-missile cruiser USS Shiloh (CG 67) as it steams past the Shiloh. Shiloh is forward-deployed to the U.S. 7th Fleet area of operations in support of security and stability in the Indo-Pacific region. (U.S. Navy photo by Mass Communication Specialist 2nd Class Ryre Arciaga)

200309-N-KW492-0096 PHILIPPINE SEA (Mar. 9, 2020) The Ticonderoga-class guided-missile cruiser USS Antietam (CG 54) transits the Philippine Sea. Antietam is forward deployed to the U.S. 7th Fleet area of operations in support of security and stability in the Indo-Pacific region. (U.S. Navy photo by Mass Communication Specialist 2nd Class Ryre Arciaga)

200310-N-KW492-0678 PHILIPPINE SEA (Mar. 10, 2020) *Sailors aboard the Ticonderoga-class guided-missile cruiser USS Shiloh (CG 67) heave a line during a replenishment-at-sea with the Fleet Replenishment Oiler USNS Pecos (T-AO 197). Shiloh is forward-deployed to the U.S. 7th Fleet area of operations in support of security and stability in the Indo-Pacific region. (U.S. Navy photo by Mass Communication Specialist 2nd Class Ryre Arciaga)*

200310-N-KW492-1051 PHILIPPINE SEA (Mar. 10, 2020) Boatswain's Mate 2nd Class Joseph Panganiban, from Fort Washington, Md., signals the distance of incoming cargo aboard the Ticonderoga-class guided-missile cruiser USS Shiloh (CG 67) during a replenishment-at-sea with the Fleet Replenishment Oiler USNS Pecos (T-AO 197). Shiloh is forward-deployed to the U.S. 7th Fleet area of operations in support of security and stability in the Indo-Pacific region. (U.S. Navy photo by Mass Communication Specialist 2nd Class Ryre Arciaga)

200310-N-KW492-1105 PHILIPPINE SEA (Mar. 10, 2020) The Arleigh Burke-class guided-missile destroyer USS Mustin (DDG 89), right, receives fuel and cargo during a replenishment-at-sea with the Fleet Replenishment Oiler USNS Pecos (T-AO 197) as the Ticonderoga-class guided-missile cruiser USS Shiloh (CG 67) pulls away. Shiloh is forward-deployed to the U.S. 7th Fleet area of operations in support of security and stability in the Indo-Pacific region. (U.S. Navy photo by Mass Communication Specialist 2nd Class Ryre Arciaga)

200310-N-KW492-0044 PHILIPPINE SEA (Mar. 10, 2020) The Ticonderoga-class guided-missile cruiser USS Shiloh (CG 67) conducts a live fire of a close in weapons system. Shiloh is forward-deployed to the U.S. 7th Fleet area of operations in support of security and stability in the Indo-Pacific region. (U.S. Navy photo by Mass Communication Specialist 2nd Class Ryre Arciaga)

200310-N-KW492-0114 PHILIPPINE SEA (Mar. 10, 2020) The Ticonderoga-class guided-missile cruiser USS Shiloh (CG 67) conducts a live fire of the ship's mark 45 5 inch gun. Shiloh is forward-deployed to the U.S. 7th Fleet area of operations in support of security and stability in the Indo-Pacific region. (U.S. Navy photo by Mass Communication Specialist 2nd Class Ryre Arciaga)

200310-N-KW492-0216 PHILIPPINE SEA (Mar. 10, 2020) Gunner's Mate 3rd Class Demarcus Gatison, from Vallejo, Ca., fires an MK38 25mm machine gun during live-fire weapons training aboard the Ticonderoga-class guided-missile cruiser USS Shiloh (CG 67). Shiloh is forward-deployed to the U.S. 7th Fleet area of operations in support of security and stability in the Indo-Pacific region. (U.S. Navy photo by Mass Communication Specialist 2nd Class Ryre Arciaga)

200311-N-KW492-0154 PHILIPPINE SEA (Mar. 11, 2020) Aviation Electrician's Mate 3rd Class Ross Perzyk, from Marysville Mich., assigned to the "Warlords" of Helicopter Maritime Strike Squadron (HSM) 51, inserts a sonar buoy into the sonar buoy launcher of an MH-60R Sea Hawk on the flight deck of the Ticonderoga-class guided-missile cruiser USS Shiloh (CG 67). Shiloh is forward deployed to the U.S. 7th Fleet area of operations in support of security and stability in the Indo-Pacific region. (U.S. Navy photo by Mass Communication Specialist 2nd Class Ryre Arciaga)

200311-N-KW492-0245 PHILIPPINE SEA (Mar. 10, 2020) Boatswain's Mate Seaman Aliana Valde, left, from New City, N.Y., removes a chain from an MH-60R Sea Hawk, assigned to the "Warlords" of Helicopter Maritime Strike Squadron (HSM) 51, as Boatswain's Mate 2nd Class Joseph Panganiban, from Fort Washington, Md., observes for safety on the flight deck of the Ticonderoga-class guided-missile cruiser USS Shiloh (CG 67). Shiloh is forward deployed to the U.S. 7th Fleet area of operations in support of security and stability in the Indo-Pacific region. (U.S. Navy photo by Mass Communication Specialist 2nd Class Ryre Arciaga)

200313-N-KW492-0118 PHILIPPINE SEA (Mar. 13, 2020) Ens. Mathew Pentaleri, from Jacksonville, Fla., monitors the SPA-25G console for surface contacts on the bridge aboard the Ticonderoga-class guided-missile cruiser USS Shiloh (CG 67). Shiloh is forward deployed to the U.S. 7th Fleet area of operations in support of security and stability in the Indo-Pacific region. (U.S. Navy photo by Mass Communication Specialist 2nd Class Ryre Arciaga)

200313-N-KW492-0031 PHILIPPINE SEA (Mar. 13, 2020) Seaman Devin Bennett, from Chesterfield, Va., reports surface contacts as he stands watch as lookout on the starboard bridge wing of the Ticonderoga-class guided-missile cruiser USS Shiloh (CG 67). Shiloh is forward deployed to the U.S. 7th Fleet area of operations in support of security and stability in the Indo-Pacific region. (U.S. Navy photo by Mass Communication Specialist 2nd Class Ryre Arciaga)